My Life is a Quilt
A Book of Quaker Messages

SOUTHEASTERN YEARLY MEETING PUBLISHING

My Life is a Quilt
A Book of Quaker Messages

Wendy Clarissa Geiger

My Life is a Quilt: A Book of Quaker Messages by Wendy Clarissa Geiger
Published by SOUTHEASTERN YEARLY MEETING PUBLICATIONS, SOUTHEASTERN YEARLY MEETING OF THE RELIGIOUS SOCIETY OF FRIENDS, nonprofit corporation founded in 1963.
www.seym.org / SEYMQuakers. org
© 2017 SEYM. All rights reserved.
Requests for permission to quote or to translate should be addressed to the author Wendy Clarissa Geiger or to SOUTHEASTERN YEARLY MEETING PUBLICATIONS.
Printed on recycled archival paper.

Cover art: *Patchwork Lives: Glory in Hues*© by Wendy Clarissa Geiger.
Content and Cover Design: Lyn Cope.
Copy Editor: Ellie Caldwell.
Author photograper: Eris A. Northern, used with permission.
Print masters: SEYM PUBLICATIONS.
Printing: Ingram Lightning Source

Cover font Avenir, French for "future," was designed by Adrian Frutiger in the late 20th c. taking inspiration from the geometric style of sans-serif typefaces created in the 1920s. Frutiger intended Avenir to be a more organic interpretation of the geometric style. Text is set in Warnock Pro© designed by Robert Slimbach for Adobe co-founder John Warnock.

eReader formats: $5.99
  ISBN 978-1-939831-24-8 (eReader: MOBI)
  ISBN 978-1-939831-25-5 (eReader: EPub)

Print: $15.00
  ISBN 978-1-939831-23-1

Contents

My life is a quilt, and Quakerism is the stitching.

The Universe is infinite; therefore, the center of God is everywhere.

—*Message given in meeting, 11/16/2002*

This book is dedicated to Jacksonville Friends Meeting, past, present, and future.

Forward

The tradition of Quakers to sit in silence and perhaps give a message in vocal ministry is a mystery in the realm of mystical spiritual life. Who dares to speak of having received a message of divine order? How is one to listen in a way that judgment does not limit hearing the message? Does vocal ministry have to be understood to have meaning? Or understood by most listeners? All these are matters to ponder while listening during meeting for worship.

Here is a collection of vocal ministry that presents similar work for the reader. Can we hear what is meant or is it unclear to us? Does clarity come at a later time? What strikes the heart and what misses the mark? And does that change?

Vocal ministry is one of the primary engines of Quaker life, especially lives amidst change and seeking. This collection is the seeking of one person hoping to encourage others. Hers is unique in that such collections are almost nonexistent. In that way this is an experiment and only a reading will decide what will follow — new tradition or old.

JOHN CALVI, Quaker Healer
Author of *The Dance Between Hope and Fear*

PREFACE

There is much in Quaker literature about vocal ministry, the relatively short messages delivered in modern Quaker unprogrammed meeting for worship. Very few transcripts of such vocal ministry can be found in print, hence this booklet of messages that have come to my heart-mind during the last 25 or so years.

Some came suddenly or subtly in meeting for worship on Sunday mornings which I either let season for a time before feeling led to deliver them aloud, or I felt my heart sink and palpitate and so delivered them forthwith — hopefully, in an audible voice. Some came suddenly or subtly any time of the day or night during the week, for which I routinely kept pen and paper with me to write them down. These messages would season in meeting for worship and were delivered when ripe. A message often appeared in my heart-mind in the same way I suddenly remembered a vegetable I had forgotten to buy at the store. It was not part of my developing train of thoughts. It usually appeared fully developed, clear, and startling.

I hope reading this booklet inspires other Quakers to write down their vocal ministry and share such messages with wider Quakerdom. For I believe the same or similar messages are being delivered in Quaker meetings around the United States of America and around the world. Sharing transcripts of vocal ministry between meetings and yearly meetings, we may see vividly our Quaker story — past, present, and future.

My Life is a Quilt
A Book of Quaker Messages

BEAUTY

You create Beauty. You revel in Beauty. You pause and honor Beauty, so that Beauty honors you. Beauty is revealed in you, and Beauty witnesses through you.

BIBLE

There is *the* Bible. Like there is *the* Godness. Then there are "bibles" as people or trees or elephants. We "read" these "bibles." A person is *a* "bible" — perhaps the only "bible" others who encounter her will "read."

CHRIST JESUS

If you know love, then you know Christ; and, if you know Christ, then you know love.

Perhaps, reading the Bible might give me much to think about, but I prefer to "read" people who read the Bible instead and see how Christ Jesus dwells in them. Jesus, I sense, is the man, and to me, Christ is the Universal God-consciousness that Jesus and the Buddha and others developed an awareness of and discovered how to express in their personalities and lives and eagerly shared with others. It continues.

Jesus isn't the only path to God. But, Christ IS the only path to God, in that Christ is that essence that can be found in each of us: that inner core of our personality and being, that "Inner Light" as Friends like to call It. Christ is our deepest hearts' desires — and THAT is the only path to God — whatever one's religion, faith, or ethics, and whatever one wants to name It. THAT CHRIST ESSENCE lights the path to and of God.

Christ language threatens some and makes others cringe. Yet the essence of Christ language is what's being sought by some who might consider calling Christ "George" instead of the word "Christ," which may for some have much emotional baggage attached.

An adult Friend works with "at risk" youth. She's tending to the lost and troubled parts of herself. She's tending to Christ's body.

B uddha is "Christ" in a different language and time and place.

I accept future generations will discover more about Jesus than what we know or theorize about him now. More writings will be discovered. I only know the truth as it has been revealed so far. I accept that Jesus is still a mystery, as my life — and my future — are still a mystery. Friends meeting for worship offers an acknowledgement of that mystery. This mystery we honor by the silent waiting in meeting for worship. This mystery will be revealed step by step, layer by layer — some small, others giant.

Jesus knew he was divine. He grew into that awareness. "Jesus" was the man. "Christ" is the timeless essence that anyone can grow into the awareness of being.

If you believe in Jesus, then you believe in the power of nonviolence.

If we are raised in a Christian context, perhaps we cling to Jesus like we cling to a parent or familiar person in a world of people. We have to leave the shore of Christianity to explore other religions. Perhaps we will put our faith in another camp, on another shore, and return to Christianity with renewed vision and faith. Perhaps we will explore other shores, other religions. Some of us never leave Christianity's shore; others explore Christianity deeply and discover religions to be on an island, and the deeper we go into one, the closer we are to the others.

We only try to make sense of what can be seen and read regarding Jesus. Otherwise, we'd give credit to his missing years. We now ignore them as not being important learning times. We try to make sense of Jesus' life with just our knowledge of some versions of his years of ministry and his far-out conception and his resurrection. They just don't make sense without considering what Jesus did during his missing years (missing from the Bible, that is).

Some feel Jesus "is the way and the life." Some feel Christ "is the way and the life." Christ is that inner core, that inner light, that of God in Jesus. That is the way: that is a universal concept. Christ Jesus. Jesus, the Christ. Christ Mohammed. Christ Sally. Christ Joe. Etc.

I may not profess to be Christian, but do not doubt my living and dying and carrying on express my understanding of that prophet's life and ministry in ways that speak as loudly and clearly as your vocal profession does.

Jesus is a Universalist.

Jesus knew and loved himself to the Core.

For some, "Jesus" is a toxic word. Just like for some, "Mother" is a toxic word. Yet for some, these are the most beloved words in a person's vocabulary.

Jesus didn't defend himself except with compassion and trust. So, why do Christians feel the need to defend Jesus or Christianity? Jesus seemed defeated time and again. Even in death. You are a Christian and promote Christianity by being compassionate. Maybe Christianity won't survive this way, but compassion will. That's the essence. As long as compassion's around, Christianity won't die. It might be called another name, but its essence will continue.

M ay Christ's wounds heal me.

—Message given in meeting, 12/4/11

J esus said he would come again. Quakers understand Jesus comes again and again and again and again. Friends attend meeting to recognize — or welcome — Jesus in our midst. We must find Jesus in any form Jesus comes in. And, during the week we carry our meeting with us.

—Message given in meeting, 11/14/10

Jesus came to mind. And, prayer came to mind. I put them together and felt a spiritual explosion inside me. Jesus prayed. Throughout the Gospels in the New Testament, it says Jesus prayed — and prayed often. From Christianity, I hear that Jesus is wise and perfect and all-knowing — like his parent, God. But, he needed to pray. So that tells me Jesus doubted and was confused and worried and needed advice from God. The picture on the wall here in the living room is of Jesus praying. Jesus prayed!

—Message given in meeting, 10/13/13

A recovering Catholic friend told me that if I went to a Catholic church this morning, I would be given a palm frond. This Palm Sunday morning (April 16th, 2000), I contemplate palm fronds and Holy Week and Easter Sunday. I imagine laying palm fronds down in His path and being Him For Whom Palm Fronds Are Laid. As a Friend, no one gives me a palm frond or the Eucharist. I lay palm fronds on the path, and I traverse that path; I am the betrayer and the betrayed; I am the dead and the resurrected.

DEATH

Death is not a defeat. It's not a sin to die.

Death is not a defeat. Jesus showed us that.

Imagine what will be said at your funeral or memorial service and live accordingly.

Death is, in ways, not a loss but an expansion.

Always live so that it is okay to die.

FAITH

You have to do a lot of practical things to pull off a miracle.

Pain and fear have the opportunity to make suffering redemptive.

A woman who used to attend meeting had a brother who wouldn't talk to her because she had left Catholicism and become a Quaker. But, that was a time of immense spiritual growth for her. Spiritual growth is, perhaps, a purpose for living, dying, and carrying on.

This came to me in the wee hours of All Saints' Day 2001 as I was being baptized with full moonlight while lying in bed:

In the Middle East, water is precious and scarce, so that's what was used for baptisms. Use whatever's precious and scarce in your experience: peace, laughter, serenity, etc. Let it wash over you, transform you, give you a sense of hope and soften your parched emotions and attitudes. You can do it anywhere, anytime.

FRIENDSHIP

You help me become myself. You have been a great shaper of my soul. You are gems I carry in my heart. I like how I feel when you come to mind.

It is always pleasant doing business with Mike Benso at Express Printing where we Geigers get our copies made and where our Meeting newsletter gets printed. Mike is a European-American man my age who is devoted to his family and to his customers. In answer to my query last week, Mike said that although he was reared Catholic, he does not attend church services on Sundays. I've thought about this a lot since then and have concluded that Mike's religion is kindness and respect and sincerity. His church is Express Printing, and he ministers to all who come through the door to do business with him. His manner reminds me of a banner I helped make at SEYM (Southeastern Yearly Meeting of the Religious Society of Friends) when I was very young that hung on a wall at our old house: "The highest form of wisdom is kindness" (*The Talmud*).

—*Meeting message printed in the September 2003 Jacksonville Friends Meeting Newsletter*

We just don't know who thinks of us after so many years, do we? We dwell in each other. Our presence shapes not just our own lives but those of others. We might be inspiration for some people. We try to live in gratitude to each encounter with another. Perhaps someone prays for us, holds us in Wholeness and Tenderness, and we just don't know it. So, make every encounter one of reverence.

In the wee hours of this morning, I awakened to the thought of two friends who are expecting soon the birth of their first child; and, that if I wasn't occupied in this current existence, I'd love to have them as parents. We choose our parents, and our parents choose us. Our parents aren't necessarily to be our best friends or worst enemies. We are to learn from them, and they from us. And, when we don't get the parenting we need from them, we might find it in others. So, in the end — of our parents' lives or of ours — there can be forgiveness. We're here to learn from each other.

— *Message given at meeting, 8/24/2003*

P art of forgiving someone is allowing that person to have a spiritual life — allowing that person to be gentle, gracious, loving, and reverent — like oneself.

—Message given in meeting, 7/13/09

A piece of paper may disappear, but our kindness doesn't disappear. Its energy is transformed into a smile for one, a hug for another, and is passed on.

GOD

WHAT IF GOD COMMANDED US TO BE HAPPY?
Isn't that the result of obeying the Ten Commandments?

You are God experiencing being human.

TWO PEOPLE LIVING TOGETHER for sixty years don't know each other fully. That goes for even one person. But, we strive to grow into knowing ourselves and each other and in comprehending God.

A FRIEND FROM PHILADELPHIA was leading a workshop at Southeastern Yearly Meeting Gathering, and she admonished a person for seeing God as "too small" (for God is much larger, she retorted). I've thought over the years how I didn't respond to that statement. I wish I had spoken up and said that I think however one comprehends God is okay with God. Some see God as incomprehensible.

Around town right now, people are praising God very quietly and very loudly. Some are praising God too loudly for some and not loudly enough for others — or for God — to hear. I just think however one comprehends and praises God is okay with God.

Y ou express God's love in your living, dying, and carrying on. How you love others is how you understand how God loves you.

I 've never heard anyone say they've outgrown the Religious Society of Friends. Friends allow God to be God and appreciate that God takes the shape and texture of each individual's sense of God.

E ach soul is another aspect of God.

God is wholeness. The Sun shines on this side of the world while the other side is in darkness. Yet, we know Earth is whole. We seek to respond to suffering and joy with wholeness.

Gravity is God's love. "Do you believe in God?" is the same as asking: "Do you believe in gravity?"

We grow into God. Our soul's work is like a masterpiece painting. Each stroke is a lesson; each layer, a lifetime. We don't paint them all at once; we let a layer dry and season before doing more. We grow into God.

I am ever trying to overcome the male, human image of God. Yet, human is how I am, so I understand the Divine Presence most comfortably through a human-like Godness.

Where is it given that we have a right to judge what is God and of God and what isn't?

Dear God, help me as I help you deliver your kin-dom on Earth.

We favor a *big* God (the bigger the better). And, we favor a *long* life (the longer the better). We judge accordingly.

When we love God and yet hate ourselves, we really love our innermost self, *That of God Within Us*. We may be relieved to know God dwells where there is love and hate and sickness and joy. Where we despise ourselves, God is loving us.

Sometimes, I sense I'm not believed by another person. God's not believed either, so why am I complaining?

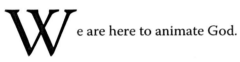

We are here to put a face on God, as are lions and frogs and mosquitoes.

We are here to animate God.

God is not "complete." God grows as we grow and as our Universe grows. We're, after all, made in God's image — as are trees and clouds and frogs and galaxies. Like God, our Universe seems humongous. But, there are probably other universes which have other gods, perhaps in other dimensions. One god per dimension? Why do we need a hierarchy of gods? Why not egalitarian gods in egalitarian dimensions?

Like sounds or light that we humans can't hear or see (though we know it's ever present), God is only sensed by humans according to what we can sense with the brain and heart. We only use 10% of our brain's capacity (or some percentage near that). So, why should we judge another's perception of God, even if that person puts restrictions on God's identifying characteristics we would not do? We may share with others our perceptions of God in order to help each other expand them.

God changes us, and we change God. God grows with the expanding Universe.

Our Father who art in Heaven...

Our Father who art in our hearts and among us (and between us).

Heaven is in our hearts (and minds). That's where God dwells: in our hearts. We share with each other only what we sense of God. Why judge another's perceptions of God?

Jesus: "No one comes to the Father except through me." The Father is God. Jesus is our innermost heart thoughts. We experience God through our hearts, in other words.

God created this world in six days. But, these were God's days — not mountains' days or humans' days or moths' days. It is all relative. How very much longer to us humans are God's days than days are for humans here in this place in this Universe. And, how very much longer is a human's day compared to a day for a moth, whose life span seems so short from a human's vantage point.

We are told to "be still and know that I am God." I more often am still and know that I am odd.

We all see God differently. Some see more than one God, like a fly's eyes see many images.

Space does not end; it is not enclosed somewhere, somehow. But, my concept of God as super-human has boundaries. Perhaps, God's message to us is: live infinity, live infinitely, or live with infinite possibilities of "God Within" and observe how the heart-mind expands infinity, expands infinitely.

We judge God's acceptance of something or someone on how accepting we are. God doesn't need us to define God's limits and relationships with us or others (especially with those with whom we disagree).

God is in the space that the Universe has yet to expand into. Therefore, God is in our dreams and the future right now.

God did not say it was perfect; God said it was good. "I am the way, the life..." means being a child of God is the way, the life.

CONTINUING REVELATION means we're not only to answer that of God in everyone, but we're, also, to ask that of God in everyone so as to expand our images of God.

HOLDING SOMEONE IN TENDERNESS AND WHOLENESS *is* doing God; it's God as a verb.

God is the maestro of the Universal Symphony.

You are God experiencing being you.

Humans are the personification of the Universe, and God is the soul of the Universe. Humans are the personification of God. Trees are the treeness of God.

Your love of God is God loving you.

God — to be God — has to experience being human, and being rock, and being cloud, and being rabbit, and being comet, and being shadow, and being night, etc, in order to be whole. And, being whole means being God.

On Friday, November 30th, 2007, the message came to me: "I am human, an aspect of All That Is; no thought is alien to me." On Sunday, December 2nd, 2007, this message was delivered in meeting for worship: "Nothing human is alien to God; nothing deer is alien to God; nothing elephant is alien to God; nothing tree is alien to God; nothing river is alien to God." Then, I was released from the message. Yet, it wasn't until the end of worship that the second part of the message came to me which I shared after worship during sharing time: "Nothing rock is alien to God; nothing waterfall is alien to God; nothing comet is alien to God; nothing alien is alien to God."

I have a friend who's dying. Carolyn and I had a marvelous conversation yesterday about her dying. Afterwards, I heard from a mutual friend that Carolyn didn't believe in God. What suddenly came to me after our conversation was, "What's more important, you believing in God? Or God believing in you?"

—Message given in meeting, 11/13/11

Believing in an all-powerful, omnipotent, omnipresent, super-human God relieves us — or gets us off the hook — of believing in humanity's human potential.

—Message given in meeting, 5/17/10

We humans need to say, "I bless you, God." Every Sunday is Father's Day for God. Every Sunday is Mother's Day for God, too.

I don't pray that God's will — and not my will — be done so much as I pray to live my life/death so that God's will and my will are the same.

—Message given in meeting, 2/18/10

Why would God demand more from us than to be totally human?

—Message given in meeting, 4/14/10

A day for God is not the same as a day for humans; and a day for moths is not the same as a day for humans. A day for humans is a whole lifetime for certain insects. So, when God created the world in six days, that is six days for God, which isn't the same as six days for humans.

In the film on nonviolence and John Dear's life and work, *The Narrow Path*, there's a line something like, "God can't protect us from terrorists blowing up the Twin Towers." God *can* protect us from terrorists blowing up the Twin Towers. Not that the Twin Towers wouldn't be destroyed. But, that God — that Inner Peace/Goodness, that Innermost Essence of Our Hearts — can transform our hatred and anxiety and anger at terrorists into compassion and understanding; and, *that* attitude/beingness saves us from destruction and from committing violence toward ourselves and others and thus protects us from terrorists.

We're here to expand each other's perimeters/concepts of Godness.
—Message given in meeting, 5/26/09

Creating art is birthing God.

God is to ocean as human lifetime is to wave. We are part of God as waves are part of ocean.

In efforts to explain our faith, we often silence God.

—Message on Monday, 5/16/11

The path of God is the way of most love.

God makes prayers out of our feebleness.

—Message given in meeting, 12/16/12

The emptiness of God means the fullness of life.

GRIEF

May our tears water the flowers along our grieving pathways.

On Sunday, December 21ˢᵗ, 2008, Jacksonville Friends Meeting for Worship followed by potluck lunch was held at the Geiger farmhouse with ten Caucasian Friends (and one Caucasian Lutheran) present. Soon after we settled into the stillness of worship, the following message came to me and wouldn't leave me alone. The hour passed quickly with the message gently, repeatedly surfacing in my heart-mind. Yet I resisted delivering it. Then, Fa announced the shift from worshiping to a short time of sharing that which we might not have felt led to share in worship (a gentle way to end meeting for worship). Soon, I stopped resisting and delivered the following message:

A little over a week ago, a dear friend's eldest son, Garrett, was shot and killed. This past week, my time was spent telephoning and e-mailing and praying (with words at times) and crying. Friday, I had a shift in consciousness regarding equality. I awakened to accepting with equal validity the gaudy plastic, mass-produced crosses or Mother Mary statuettes on car dashboards and the simply elegant, hand-carved olivewood crosses or Nativity sets. All images of holiness serve to heighten awareness of the sacred. My heart quickens at the thought of all of these images now that are equal conduits of Truth. During worship, the realization came to me that this new awareness is a gift from Garrett. May we hold in Tenderness and Wholeness Garrett and his Family.

Happiness

Why do we adamantly pursue happiness in this society, and at what cost?

HEAVEN

For some, heaven is a place where we will have no worries, problems, hardships, or heartaches. Heaven does not have these things only because when they arise, we'll know how to constructively and peacefully deal with them, so they don't overwhelm us and leave us feeling helpless and unhealthy. In heaven, we'll be helpful with each other in dealing with these things in healthy ways.

Meryl Streep, the European-American actress, was asked: "What would God say about heaven?" She answered, "Everyone in." Do we feel this way about our own hearts? Are we welcoming of everyone in our own hearts? Our hearts are our very own heaven — our practice heaven, if you will. Do we say, "George W. Bush in"? Do we say, "Saddam Hussein in"? Do we say, "Everyone in" in our own hearts?

You know paradise. You carry it in your heart.

Why are we supposed to live to ripe old ages? What would heaven be like if only elders were there? Heaven is a lot like Earth; it's just we'll know how to creatively, constructively deal with conflicts then.

Reincarnation is habit forming.

HELL

Being told, "Go to Hell!" is a deep honor. Going to Hell is our great task as peacemakers. We must record and share what Hell is. For so many in Hell — or who have witnessed Hell — are speechless. They are dead soldiers, veterans, and traumatized people around the globe. We can speak for these people and bear witness to their Hell and claim it as ours. Going to Hell, one knows the struggle, the injustices, and the intolerable conditions of our brothers and sisters throughout the world. Going to Hell, we enter into their suffering, their misery, their confusion and their pain, and share these conditions through trying to understand them. We thus let the sufferer know she or he is not alone. For alone — without Spirit or without fleshly companions — is Hell.

For we are their brothers and sisters and can do something about it in our land and with our resources. We must articulate our vision of the possible future of Heaven-on-Earth for those living in abject poverty and extreme wealth and for those who do not speak or choose not to speak of Hell.

We're getting a glimpse of the emotional state of the one who tells us to "go to Hell." That call is a plea to feel what they're feeling, to be a companion in their pain. European-American Friend Cathy Gaskill stated during a meeting for business at a Southeastern Yearly Meeting Gathering: "Some say Quakers are going to Hell. That's true. Quakers *are* going to Hell. Because Quakers are needed in Hell, and we go where we're needed."

Going to Hell offers us an opportunity for living with compassion and connection. It means going to the place where I now dwell in my anger and acrimony, so you can feel how I now feel. Share with me so I will not be alone.

INTEGRITY

Have no enemy but falsehood.

A friend noted that a newspaper columnist took Qur'an quotes out of context. Their meanings change when the sentences before and after them are not included. We judge our lives and those of others out of context; we don't include experiences and attitudes of other lifetimes — or even those of our current lifetimes.

I n this society we are encouraged to cheat. Have same result easier, faster, with less hassle, with less work. Ah, there: less time and work — same output. But, an artist takes time for her or his job. We gaze at a painting by Gullah artist Jonathan Green, for instance, and admire the time spent to please us and himself, the thousands of deliberate brush strokes. His painting style embodies respect, deep respect for himself, his subject matter (Gullah culture), and the viewer.

I n calling people names — such as "Christian" or "Quaker" — we accept or reject a label according to our perceptions of ourselves and/or others. We are — or, are not — fitting of given labels. Labels give us reference points on our journeys through life and death. They give us structures to stand or climb on so as to see or feel different or view new perspectives.

The purpose of life is to protect joy.

Quakers don't swear an oath in court because we tell the truth at all times. Likewise, why do we call God to be in our midst when God is always present?

Americans are very demanding of God since 9/11/01. So, may we hold God in the Light.

—Message given in meeting on Veterans Day

LOVE

"LOVE ONE ANOTHER AS I HAVE LOVED YOU," said Christ Jesus. He freed us to love everybody, as he loved all people.

Society tells us we are not worthy of God's love (the Universe's love). Therefore, we are not worthy of loving ourselves. It is not worth the effort. Even if we try, we will still be just as unlovable afterwards. Jesus taught us to love and respect ourselves.

L ove is like light; it enters wherever there is a crack or door ajar. If you can't love yourself, maybe you can love one other person. Then you can find you love another. If you can't love another, perhaps you can love a work of art or an animal or a mathematical formula or a sunset or a memory or a sweater. You can begin somewhere and practice loving. And, once you open your heart to loving one thing, then another, you may eventually find yourself enjoying how loving makes you feel.

S ome people *love* to hate.

Jesus had an all-encompassing love for everybody — which means everybody who ever lived and will live. That's how we know he loves us, now and in the future. When we love, it penetrates the ages of time and spaces of our Universe. Love is the energy fueling the Universe that we tap into anywhere, anytime. It's self-generating.

Those who cause us grief are gifts so that we can practice loving the enemy.

If we can only love others as much as we love ourselves, then perhaps we can only believe Jesus is divine as much as we believe we too are divine.

Make a world welcoming and worthy of the unborn.

We will not be judged by how we lived, but by how we loved. We actually won't be judged in the sense that we commonly think of it: distributing and meting out punishment or proclaiming and finding someone guilty or innocent of a crime. We will just be more aware and awake and see a bigger picture than before death. Our horizons keep expanding. We are not just seeing with our two eyes in the front of our heads; we are "seeing" with our memories of other dimensions and views. We gain understanding through touch and smell and hearing, too. We will judge ourselves on how much we have changed in order to know what lessons we need to learn in the future and have learned in the past.

 My heart surrounds you all with love.

At the start of centering down, I asked God how to deal with Friends United Meeting Friends and attitudes, and immediately the response was: "Love, as angels love."

Being outside Christianity means being with the dispossessed of life — means being in hell — means bringing love where there's hate or indifference.

NATURE

The tree trunk is the soul. The branch is a lifetime. The leaves are lessons. And, the roots are God: nourishment not always visible unless one searches for it — yet always there.

Our lifetimes and lives are like plants: some straight and narrow like asparagus; some exuberant like collards; some with children like fruit trees; and, some intense like broccoli. As we grow, we branch out — with relationships and thoughts — like tree limbs. We may glean wisdom from one tradition like some trees get nourishment from single taproots; while at other times we glean wisdom from many sources like elaborate root systems of some trees. Even a straight and tall tree with few branches does not represent all trees. Because it is tall, does that mean "better"? Because it is old and gnarly, does that mean "better"? Why is a tree supposed to be best when it grows tall or lives for a long time? Same with people.

What's a favorite spiritual practice? Watching rain fall is the answer: being present to the rain, giving it attention, recognizing its egalitarian nature, and recognizing its cleansing nature. Rain — everyone gets a little or a lot of it at a given time. It's a blessing or a curse. It's nourishing, a necessity. It's holy and pure and polluted.

The birds sing the morning into being.

Trees are like humans: roots not seen. Trees get nurturing from the sun through leaves and rain through roots. Some of our life is interior — like roots of trees are underground.

Some plant seeds only germinate and travel if digested and excreted by animals. Some plant seeds have a wing or wings attached or fluff attached, so the seeds will travel far and wide, drawn aloft by the wind. Other seeds have burrs attached, to spread afar by clinging to animal fur or humans' pants. And, seeds of wisdom uttered by humans spread by way of the love "attached" to them. Whatever we utter becomes seeds. Some of these seeds fail to be heard. Some of these seeds are heard but not understood or are forgotten. Some of these seeds are nourished in our heart-minds and develop into food for the soul — for our souls and for others' souls.

—Message given in meeting, 5/2/10

PEACE

How can you know peace if you don't, also, know struggle? Both were conditions present in the womb in which you were carried.

We are healthy when our bodies are Peaceable Kingdoms.

If you have peace, then do you also, with that, have joy? Vice versa, when you experience joy, you must cultivate even a moment of peace.

Respect toward youth by older people begins by ridding Earth of nuclear weapons and war.

Do what you love; the peace will follow. Do the justice; the peace will follow.

Nonviolence is often the norm of life; we just do not call it that.

Peace is an attitude of the heart.

—Message given in meeting, 8/5/10

Oh, we need the inspiration! We need to feel the longings of the world toward Peace!

—Message given in meeting, 8/4/07

PERSONALITY

A person's personality is like a state or a country. One might be cold and full of highs and lows or rather dry with areas lush and verdant. Another might be like the English countryside. Another like the United States with a wide variety of personality traits. A person's personality might have boundaries like a state or country. One might be well-defined while another melds with a neighboring personality.

Intellectuals should try not to see intellectualism as a superior trait. Perhaps a person's sole/soul purpose in this lifetime is to experience kindness — giving and receiving it — and intellectualism isn't necessary; compassion is. Or maybe, we're ornery and mean in a lifetime. This gives others opportunities to practice peacemaking and lovingkindness in hard circumstances.

G od is the soul of this Universe. When we feel we're not in touch with God, it's not that we aren't "in touch," but it's just that we're *unaware* of such a relationship. It's like when we feel — personally — that we're bogged down in the nitty-gritty of living and aren't in touch with or aware of our own psychological needs: we need bread, but we need roses, too. Take care of the physical body, but also, the mind.

Y our gift to someone is your attention to them.

I could give you a good luck coin to keep in your pocket on your trip. But if you lose it, you'd know you're still in luck, because it's the attention, intention, and the psychic quality that is the true gift behind the coin, an outward manifestation. The coin is just a reminder of the luck wish.

We live in a culture of absolutes and certainty. We are not supposed to be uncertain or say, "I don't know." At age 18, I decided I didn't know much of anything. Even when I think I do, I catch myself and change my mind, and that opens me to new possibilities, new thinking, new realities.

I am a spiritual materialist.

Quakers are all types, symbolic of a person's life: the questioner, the believer, the doubter, the debt collector. Sometimes we're more one way than another.

—Message I didn't deliver during Easter worship
at SEYM Gathering 2009, but delivered later

PRAYER

The Caucasian Rabbi Abraham Joshua Heschel said after marching with Martin Luther King Jr. and others, "I felt my legs were praying." When we see God in other people and other entities, then our eyes are praying. When we love others, then our hearts are praying.

—*Message given at meeting, 7/22/01*

Appreciating a flower is prayer.

E ven if you don't think of it as prayer, organizing your thoughts and pleas to yourself in a coherent way is bound to be good for your system, your understanding of this Universe. It's prayer for some.

P rayer opens up the future for the pray-er. Praying is envisioning the future.

P rayer is internal action.

Holding someone in the Light, I imagine the Light burning off old baggage the person carries, and the Light burning off the buildup of misunderstandings. Holding someone in the Light brings forth an image of the person's path being illumined or cleared so that person can see choices of possible futures available.

While centering down in meeting, I began to silently pray, "Dear God, please… ." After I listed several requests, God calmly interrupted me with: "I am here. Be here, also." So, I returned to praying without agenda.

—This message is part of the first paragraph in my "Voices and Visions" essay that appeared in the November 2004 issue of Jacksonville Meeting's newsletter.

Christmas is a prayer of the heart.

—Message given in meeting, 8/6/10

My love for you all is a prayer.

I am hallowed by Thy name. Thy kin-dom well up from within. My kin-dom come to my well being dug. Unearth what is my inner heaven.

QUAKERISM

My life is a quilt, and Quakerism is the stitching.

From the earliest days of Quakerism, we have heard to "walk cheerfully over the Earth answering that of God in everyone" (George Fox). Alice Walker, the African-American writer, wrote that she doesn't go to church to discover God as much as share God. I come to meeting to discover God within me. And, I go out into the world and find that of God within me reflected in others I encounter.

—*Message given at meeting, 9/2/01*

We are not followers of Jesus. We are Friends of Jesus.

Some Quakers hold weekly pep rallies for God. Other Quakers stage concerts and theater performances — hoping to please God. The unprogrammed branches of Quakerism have forgone the pep rallies and instead have chosen — or been led — to sit quietly in expectant waiting for an hour of worship to pray and invite God into a weekly collective interior cleaning party, quietly dusting and polishing and cleaning inner windows, doors, walls, and furnishings.

Friends carry our religion within. My religion is compassion.

Among unprogrammed Friends, the Bible is used alongside other spiritual writings. It's not that Quakers don't revere the Bible as much as it is revered among other religious bodies. It's like having more than one child. A parent doesn't love the first one less than the others. Love comes abundantly for all.

Most Christian denominations have creeds that shape you as a member. You must conform to the way members view God; the creeds define and confine God. As for Quakerism, in the silence we try to discern how God shapes us, how our deepest inner self is expressed as God. We try not to confine God or define God in God's entirety with our limited vision. The Quaker family tree has many branches. Some talk to each other; some don't. Some don't believe others' beliefs; some do. All started from the same roots and are reaching for the same God/Sun.

Christocentric and Universalist Friends are not an either/or identity. Universalism includes Christocentricity. Universalist Friends just don't stop at Jesus, but include Buddha and Mohammed and saints, etc. Universalists don't ignore Jesus; they include Jesus, but they just don't make him their exclusive teacher.

I love George Fox's alleged suggestion to William Penn that he wear his sword as long as he could. We keep our beliefs for as long as we can.

I've thought of separations and schisms in Quakerdom of yesteryear as being negative, things to avoid. Now, I think differently. Whether it is the life of an individual or of a community or family, separations and schisms — and sometimes reconciliations — happen. They are natural occurrences as individuals and groups grow. A person's life isn't straight and narrow or wide. There are twists and turns and crossroads to choose from — either or both ways — along the journey for individuals and groups of all sizes.

When I "hold someone in the Light," I visualize that person illumined and her situation and her problem illumined, too. It's a process of lighting the path for that person so that she can see herself, her problem, and its possible solutions with greater clarity and understanding than before. The darkness is perfect for resting, for incubating, for rejuvenating. That person's light might be so blocked or dim at times, she needs us to hold our inner lamps near her, to share warmth, to encourage her, and to affirm her presence.

Why do some "liberal" Friends think Catholics or Buddhists are our brothers and sisters but not evangelical Friends? Do I allow evangelical Friends a spiritual life? The good news is that Christ will outlast Christianity. Thank God!

Unprogrammed Friends "clean" our inner sanctuaries on First Day in meeting for worship. Then, we go out in the world during the week, offering our presence to people and animals and trees, and perhaps offering clarity, care, and respite.

Unprogrammed Quakers carry on the traditions of George Fox and Margaret Fell — as do Friends United Meeting Quakers — just as Southern Baptists carry on traditions of Jesus: the enthusiasm and joy of Jesus, the love of Jesus and God. And, unprogrammed Quakers carry on traditions of Jesus in other ways.

go by churches with many cars in their parking lots. They offer a lot of answers — easy to image or imagine. Quaker meeting offers the vastness of inner and outer space to formulate our own goodness. There are beacons burning brightly or dimly to guide the way — not even that, because there's no *one* way. But, the beacons — our Inner Lights sitting in the circle, our scriptures of Quakerism, the Bible — shine enough light for us to recognize our own divinity and the divinity amongst us.

—Message given in meeting, 2/11

great gift of Quakerism is cultivating the feeling I'm neither superior nor inferior to anyone or anything in the entire Universe.

—Message given in meeting, 2/19/12

SILENCE

Trust the silent places in others' lives. Trust they are significant to their growth.

Quakers recognize, cultivate, accept, and frame silence like a clear view of the mountains. We don't build a pagoda symbolizing something. We just use silence — as free as the air. We stand up for silence. We advertise silence by being translucent ourselves. Silence is our companion, an extension of us created anywhere, anytime. I see an image of the Peace Pagoda being built next to the Smoky Mountains by Buddhist friends and others. Why can't we feel the peace and awe just by looking at the mountains without the pagoda in the way? Do we need a peace pagoda? A blade of grass or a mountain would work just as well. Yet the pagoda is a monument to humans' willingness and capacity to strive for peace.

During meeting for worship, is a message from out of the Silence? Or is it a message held within the Silence and then released?

I am connected in the silence with all those who choose silence as a spiritual gift and all those who are condemned to silence.

—What came to me in the silence as we began Southeastern Yearly Meeting Worship & Ministry Committee's conference phone call, 9/30/10

SIMPLICITY

A simple life means having few enemies.

—Message given in meeting, 7/10

L ife is a query.

SOCIAL CONSCIOUSNESS

I hear and see people say and write how "lucky" we are to live in the USA, and that we shouldn't complain because we have it so good and so much better than so many folk in the world. It's not luck, we must tell them. It's planned, and it's greed that creates our lifestyles. Think of all we've thieved from the impoverished "unlucky" ones.

Martin Luther King Jr. Parkway in Jacksonville now finally has signs up. Consider the inconvenience of it all to businesses, having to change stationery, business cards, and receipts! Similarly, Martin Luther King Jr. was an "inconvenient hero," as Vincent Harding, the historian of the African-American experience, calls him.

—Message given at meeting on Christmas Eve morning

Meeting for worship is inconvenient: the discipline of a long period of silence and having to inspire oneself and the rest of meeting. It takes thinking and praying and is a lot of work. Being a Quaker is inconvenient. Jesus was the ultimate inconvenient hero. As Thomas Merton wrote, "Into this world, this demented inn, in which there is absolutely no room for him at all, Christ has come uninvited."

We feel we MUST share in others' suffering while helping to relieve that suffering. To help someone up out of the mud, one needs firm footing, a solid base. It's the same with helping to relieve suffering. But, it helps the sufferers if they know those who aren't suffering are aware of their plight, feel their suffering, too.

R acism colors everything.

Just because Quakers were against slavery doesn't mean modern Quakers are working on our racism when we proclaim ourselves to be anti-racist. Anti-slavery doesn't translate into anti-racism.

Y ou have no idea the forces opposing the celebration of Black History Month. It is like trying to walk through molasses. Celebrating Black History Month goes against all that this society deems the steps to success. It is honoring what this society still deems dishonorable. It is the powerful act of publicly witnessing to memories, and publicly evoking love, honor, and truth where there has been indifference, shame, and misinformation. Future generations will scarcely comprehend why this society only acknowledged Black history for one month — the shortest and the coldest one at that. Black history will be taught in every school and grade level. Acknowledging, celebrating, or commemorating Black history makes it real — whether or not society dismisses and discredits its importance. We will proudly recall our parts in creating history by participating in Florida State College at Jacksonville's Black History Month events.

We are an advanced civilization, but how advanced can we be when we are threatening all of life with nuclear annihilation and extinction?

Why is "Please Call Me By My True Names" by Thich Nhat Hanh my favorite poem? I must remember — as a peace activist — the militarist within: that which is rigid, on guard, ready to kill without thinking, ready to kill, period. Kill: with words, with tone of voice, with my eyes. Kill people. Kill ideas. That's violence: my willingness to judge the militarist, my willingness to condemn the militarist, anybody really, my willingness to see the militarist as "other than me," as the enemy. But, at the same time, the militarist *is* my opposition. She or he is the person I'm trying to convert. She or he dwells, also, within me. She or he is not the enemy. No. The enemy is violence.

Maybe I do not have physical ancestors who were African American or Latina/o, but I can claim spiritual Ancestors of Color.

Every life is a success. Even the homeless derelict of a person sprawled on a street corner passed out or not even able to beg for money — even that person's life is a success in that he offers those who pass him by the opportunity to practice compassion.

Americanism says, "You have a right to be comfortable." Christianity says, "It is right to be comforting."

—Message given in meeting, 10/21/01, soon after 9/11/01

The Christian will be uncomfortable — but will be comforted.

—Message given at meeting, 4/07

I'm not asking men to give up power. I'm asking men to give up illegitimate power.

I've come to the conclusion that playing with war toys is playing — or practicing — war; and, playing with dinosaurs is playing — or practicing — extinction. The popularity of dinosaurs scares me. Children are preparing for extinction.

When you are a refugee or constantly on the go, may you be rooted in the Spirit.

You are worthy of a future, and the future is worthy of peace with justice.

Soul

We do everything for the advancement — or the awakening into awareness — of our own souls and selves. Each lesson — and each life we live — awaken more of us to ourselves, to our Godness.

We grow our own souls.

You are an expression of your soul.

One's soul is shaped by the truthfulness of one's life.

Honor your souls.

Universe

So many people on this Earth trust in a single God; perhaps this is due to the fact that there is only one Sun in our Solar System.

Trees are the treeness of God/the Universe.

We are the personification of the Universe, and God is the soul of the Universe.

God is the soul of this Universe. Like each of us has a soul (and a body this time 'round), this Universe has a soul.

God is the animator of this Universe.

You think with your global mind. You feel your global heartbeat. You do your work in response to hearing Earth's heartbeat.

There is love in the Universe.

In U.S. society, do we think we're alone because we're the only inhabitable planet in our solar system — and the only inhabitable planet we know of? Do we have only one God because we have only one moon and only one Sun in our solar system? Thus it would make sense that there is only one God, and that we are, first of all, individuals — independent individuals, no less. God is like the Sun.

We are asked to embrace the world with our hearts.

We are the first human beings of any century so far who are aware of international events so soon after they happen. And, we are aware of other cultures — the presence of other cultures — but maybe not that their hopes and dreams are just like our own. Differences instead of similarities are emphasized. We attend meeting for worship because we love the world and want to understand other cultures.

What makes our little Planet Earth beautiful is that there are so many opportunities to express compassion.

How can God be permanent, unchanging, in an impermanent and changing Universe (which is God creating Itself)?

The water is really one ocean on Planet Earth. We call the different areas Atlantic Ocean and Indian Ocean and Pacific Ocean. But really, it is all one body of water. Like all people are one body of God. Why don't we differentiate the air we breathe?

We know how fragile this Planet Earth is, so why do I think I'm not just as fragile, adaptable, beautiful, just as solid, just as fluid, fiery, and icy?

Recognizing Earth Day is celebrating the Universe expressing Itself as Planet Earth. Recognizing Mother's Day is celebrating the Universe expressing Itself as motherhood in all its forms on Planet Earth and Elsewhere.

Let my heart (God) encompass the Universe.

Our planetary system has only *one* star at its center. I've heard it's more common for stars to be binary. Perhaps, that's why so many religions have a *single* primary god (or goddess). Because we have only *one* sun.

The Universe is infinite; therefore, the center of God is everywhere.

—Message given at meeting, 11/16/02

WHOLENESS

We are whole. We just focus on one or a few aspects of our whole personality in one lifetime — like one focuses on one step at a time on a journey or one task at a time in doing chores. If we're mentally ill in this lifetime, we're still whole because wholeness is a completeness of lifetimes. We only see a portion of our personality at a given time — like seeing only part of the moon at a given time. But, we know the moon to be a whole orb.

Each of us has our own journey and lessons to learn in a dance with others. We are whole — each of us; yet we are exploring our own wholeness (which includes many lifetimes of experiences) and the wholeness of humanity and the wholeness of the Earth Community, too.

While we may see ourselves as broken, other friends may see us as whole. And, while we struggle, others are holding us in Wholeness and Tenderness.

Deep sorrow hollows out a place for deep joy to abide in one's life. Perhaps, one's whole life is expressed in deep sorrow. Yet, in another lifetime, one may feel an eternity of deep joy. It all balances out.

We look back to when we were babies, and we say we were perfect then. Perhaps, for the rest of our lives, we explore that perfection — or wholeness.

WORSHIP

The process of meeting for worship…waiting…waiting… . Waiting is what poor people do. Poor in spirit, perhaps, are we? I think of early Friends in England and in this country. What did they do to prepare for meeting for worship? How did they conduct their daily lives? Or, did God do the conducting, and they played the music?

It is so appropriate for Friends to worship in a school library, as we do here in Jacksonville. We open ourselves to ideas and the word of God during the silence of worship — like students open these books and study the words on the pages.

—Message given at meeting, 7/1/01

The Cathedral Church of St. John the Divine in New York City is a womb of God. It inspires and envelops. This library is a womb of God. It inspires and envelops us. We don't read these books. We "read" each other and others who we encounter.

—Message given at meeting, 7/29/01

"**G**o forth in joy," the cleric says to his congregation at the end of the worship service. The church is where we gather each Sunday and enter our inner sanctums of ourselves: where we are at home, where we experience awe and rejuvenate our spirits, our emotional and mental attitudes. When we physically dwell for an hour or more a week in a sanctuary — perhaps, the only sanctuary we know — with others who may think like we do and tend to share our values, we know the potential for our daily private meditation and appreciation time. Joining with others in a congregation each Sunday for services reinforces our knowing that we are not alone in our exploring and seeking goodness and joy in our living, dying, and carrying on.

The paper matter and books I collect and save are testaments and evidence of support for my values and beliefs. And, on First Day (Sunday) morning, I come to meeting with Quaker literature, but during meeting for worship, I don't hold them or read them or place them in the center of the circle. They remain outside the circle on a table. We come to meeting to be vessels of Godness, not to prove our beliefs are right or wrong, but to ruminate on openness and put our beliefs aside for a time of inner gardening, one with another.

Religion is from where we get such great strength. Yet it is, also, where we can feel most vulnerable.

We would never laugh at a child because she or he could only crawl and not walk or run. So, why dismiss someone's manner of worship or prayer because it is not as "mature" as our own?

Do I enter the library (where Jacksonville Friends worship) together and see within myself and other Friends the awesomeness of God as I do when I enter the Cathedrals of St. Patrick and St. John the Divine in New York City and see those awesome structures and stained glass windows and the immensity of those holy places? Yet, most of these places are made of air, of "empty" space contained in these buildings. But, the emptiness is filled with love and sorrow and despondency and awe and happiness and holiness and other thoughts and feelings of the parishioners and visitors. God's presence there made these prayers and thoughts and feelings and people held between the walls and ceilings and floors blessed with Compassionate Understanding.

When I was young and sitting in meeting for worship, I was swinging my legs back and forth under the chair, making noise each time my shoes touched the floor. After a little while, Bill Greenleaf reached over and gently touched my leg. That was meant to stop me from making noise, but more importantly, it meant I was not to be bored in meeting for worship. As a carpenter goes to a jobsite prepared, so Friends come to meeting prepared. We are not to be bored and make noise and swing our legs under our chairs.

Reading thick memoirs and biographies of John Lewis, Frederick Douglass, and W.E.B. DuBois, one learns all about another's life — his living, dying, and carrying on; and, in ways, one gets to know about *all* people. And, I get to know about my own self by going into Silence for an hour once a week with other people present doing perhaps similarly, in meeting for worship.

Quaker silent worship validates the silent, invisible, rich reality of our inner lives.

Friends go to meeting to listen to God, not to entertain God.

Once, a dear friend asked me how to pray. He's the Episcopalian — and he's asking ME? But there is something about participating in meeting for worship First Day after First Day that brings to my life an all-encompassing covenant with Indonesians and grasshoppers in my yard and Laplanders and sloths of the Amazon and Joshua trees that refuse to grow near the Nevada Test Site and the Pope and those homeless and imprisoned Vietnam veterans in this nation. There is that sense of being part of all their — or our — living, dying, and carrying on. It is renewed and shaped in meeting for worship each First Day. We are all aspects of God. And, this covenant is a living prayer.

Perhaps even when meeting isn't very stimulating, the experience of meeting prepares us to feel stimulated by small, seemingly insignificant things during the rest of the week. Like building an ever-expanding clay pinch pot, meeting for worship expands our hearts week by week so that during the time between First Days, we are ever expanding our capacity for compassion and grace, love and forgiveness, silence, and awe.

In most meeting houses, benches face each other instead of facing all in one direction (toward the altar). For Friends, the altar is within us.

—*Message given in meeting, 10/16/06*

Dear Stetson (Kennedy), I gave a message at meeting this morning. I shared news of your heart attack and said there was a 99% blockage of an artery. And, I come to meeting each week to unblock my heart. I come to meeting to repair and tend to my heart from the stresses, strains, and damages of the previous week. Friends were asked to hold you in the Light and in Tenderness and Wholeness. This is the first Quaker meeting I've participated in during which I spent the whole time holding you in healing light. All my love and then some more to you and Sandra,

—Wendy

Entering a cathedral or a religious sanctuary is entering my heart: a place of prayer, of adoration, of awe, of healing — central to one's life. Like one's heart is central to one's life.

In meeting for worship we listen to what God asks of and needs from us.

I don't come to meeting to *worship* God. As a Quaker, I believe in equality. So, God is equal to anything else in the Universe. To worship any *thing* is to put that thing above myself, where I cannot view it on an equal footing. Perhaps I come to meeting to recognize God, to commune with God, to understand God, and to revel in God.

The Quaker Experiment
of Meeting For Worship

Wendy Clarissa Geiger
07/02/2016

I want this book to be open to newcomers and folk who've never heard of Quakers except seeing the guy on the oats' box. It can just simply be a devotional for folk who may not be otherwise interested in Quakers/ism.

Lovingly, Wendiferous

This evening, I read some of Howard Thurman's writings collected in the marvelous volume, *Black Fire: African American Quakers on Spirituality and Human Rights.* Howard Thurman so eloquently describes Quaker meeting for worship that when reading it "my heart did leap for joy," as George Fox, the founder of Quakerism, would attest to. Actually, perhaps, Quakerism was founded by that of "Christ within" the first Friends and perpetually is recreated within each of us as we sit in the stillness of meeting for worship on Sunday mornings and as we commune with Godde and one another — an aspect of Godde being the sacred center of our is-ness, ourselves.

125

Friends have an Integrity Testimony. At age 13, I decided to tell the truth from then on and not lie. This is a spiritual practice that affects every aspect of my living, dying, and carrying on. Someone once asked me what the basis of my spirituality is. "Being honest" was my answer. Perhaps another way of looking at that is: being awake, being aware. During meeting for worship Sunday mornings, Friends engage within ourselves in the stillness and take fierce inventory of our lives. How honest are we with ourselves and others? As we strive to live with integrity at our core of all we are and do, we try to live from the centrality of being good: to ourselves, to one another, and to Planet Earth.

Meeting for worship is an hour of forgiving ourselves and others, of pondering the previous week or the coming week, and being open to what we could've done or might do differently than previously imagined. It's a supportive hour of being open to possibilities of strengths and weaknesses we may not have been aware of, so noisy and busy our lives might be otherwise.

Friends, another term for "Quakers" (aka Religious Society of Friends), claim we listen for or to Godde in meeting for worship (what Friends call our worship service). Once in a very long time, I hear an actual Voice. Most times, a thought that came Out Of Nowhere (another name for Godde, as I see It) is pondered and nurtured, and I see if it keeps popping up in my heart-mind and won't leave me alone. I wonder if it's a message just for me or if it's for someone or more in meeting for worship? To share that Sunday or share another time? Usually, only a few (at most) messages (another term is "vocal ministry") are delivered in a given meeting for worship. Sometimes, a theme emerges that connects them. I've sung songs as vocal ministry. I've delivered messages anywhere from a few words to several minutes in length — hopefully in an audible voice. I sometimes feel an urge, sometimes a mental nudge, sometimes a sinking belly and/or a palpitating heart, sometimes a wisp of an affirmation to give a message in meeting. Some meetings are filled with silence and are spiritually juicy; and, some meetings seem "empty" with silence, as if "nothing" happened during the hour. Yet, either way, I usually feel refreshed upon returning home from meeting for worship.

Meeting for worship is a communal experiment in being open to possibilities each Sunday. Friends say we have done away with the laity, and we are all clergy, all ministering to one another. But, some Sundays I don't feel up to the task. I want a choir to inspire me, a pastor to instruct me, and plenty of warm bodies all around to affirm that (a) I'm on the right path and (b) all those gathered experienced the same thing I did, and (c) we're on the same wave-length or believe the same thing — a creed of sorts. Oh, well, Friends pride ourselves on being creedless.

For some Friends, half of meeting for worship is spent wondering if we're doing meeting for worship correctly. We're wondering if we left the stove on at home. We're deep in prayer when suddenly we remember we need to stop at the store for toothpaste on our way home. Our minds are full of images of what could have been. And, then, we discover we've made some peace with one of those could-have-been images. We see that what we did in a difficult situation last week really was the best decision given the circumstances, and that gives us a feeling of being good. Friends restore our goodness — our Original Blessing — in meeting for worship, each Sunday. We take the hour of meeting for worship on Sunday morning to clean the windowpanes of our hearts in order for Godde to flow in and out of our hearts easily.

Friends dissect our lives, our struggles, in meeting for worship; and, we put our lives back together and we heal ourselves in meeting for worship. Since there are, usually, no external noises that distract us, Friends become friends with our heart-thoughts. They can be distracting; so, just let them be and eventually, they'll be less and less distracting. Don't give up! Sitting quietly with others doing the same encourages us to delve deep into our heart-thoughts. Or not. Friends are a brave lot. We challenge ourselves to be good residents of Planet Earth. We bring to meeting for worship our quests for Tenderness and Wholeness in our broken-ness and in the brokenness of society of which we Friends are a part.

We seek and cultivate enough beauty, hope, and joy in our lives to protect us from numbing despair when that happens to us. In a strange, marvelous, mystical way (the way of Godde), Friends have found time and time again that loving-kindness is the solution, whatever the questions, whatever the despairing situations Friends find ourselves in — within our own lives and within the lives of "our neighbors," wherever in the world "our neighbors" dwell. Some ministers advise their congregants to avoid Hell. Friends, "armed" with love, seek to transform Hell into Heaven-on-Earth. We seek to transform the Hell within us into Heaven within us by loving and forgiving. That is a wondrous experiment Friends cultivate in our lives — especially, in meeting for worship. If we are all Godde's children, then we look out for our siblings. So often, answers — or, better questions — are revealed to us in meeting for worship. An answer may come to us Out Of the Blue (there's Godde again) in our heart-thoughts, in our own vocal ministry, in the vocal ministry of another Friend, in an announcement after meeting for worship has ended, or in a tender affirmation in a conversation at the rise of meeting while Friends are socializing.

Friends use the term "a leading" — what others may term "a calling". Friends are obliged to "test" our leadings for support of the Meeting (a church) or non-support of the Meeting. Friends are expected to follow the Meeting's decision that has been discerned with Godde's help in meeting for (worship with attention to) business, which usually happens once a month. Some leadings are bold and daring and on a grand scale and take decades to accomplish with many Friends and non-Friends joining in the struggle for peace and/or justice. Some leadings are on a small scale and are accomplished relatively quickly by one Friend or one Meeting. Some Friends proclaimed slavery wrong — when slavery was so entrenched in our society and in the Religious Society of Friends — more than a century before the Emancipation Proclamation. Now, some Friends (and others) are proclaiming war is obsolete and will end — when war and war preparing is so entrenched in our society. If we can imagine it…, it can happen.

I plan to have a t-shirt made with these (bumper sticker) messages on the front and back: "Honor Veterans — No More War" and "Why is there always money for war but not for education?"

We're trusting that in sitting together in stillness for an hour, something — something — happens within us, collectively and individually, that is beyond our reasoning minds. I cannot rationally explain a typical happening in meetings across the country. For example, five or more years ago, in the middle of meeting for worship here in Jacksonville, I opened my eyes to see Friend Noel Palmer four seats away fingering pages of his Bible. I thought at that moment, I must ask Noel where in the Bible is "In my Father's house there are many mansions". Later in meeting, Noel delivered his vocal ministry and read from the Bible, "In my Father's house there are many mansions… ."

Basically, Friends experiment with our heart-minds in meeting for worship and see what love will do and be in the world through us, collectively and individually. Just as we are only human in relation to other humans, we are only Quakers in relation to other Quakers. Quakers are Quakers by sitting still in meeting for worship on Sunday mornings, again and again, come what may (or may not). Might you join the experiment?

REFERENCE

See: *quakerfinder.org* to find a Quaker meeting or worship group near you.

About the Author

Wendy Clarissa Geiger is a European-American (white) Quaker womun mystic, poet, archivist, philosopher, contemplative, activist, folksinger, artist, baker of cookies, encourager, reader, letter writer, racism awareness worker, and practitioner of love, nonviolence, and amazement as she holds the world's joys and sorrows in her heart-mind. She lives on the family farmstead in Jacksonville, Florida. She's the niece, daughter, and cousin of seven conscientious objectors to wars spanning World War II, Korea, and Vietnam. In 1959, her parents met in the Movement to Make Democracy Real, as Vincent Harding called the Civil Rights Movement. Wendy went on her first demonstration in her mother's womb in 1963, and she continuously has been involved in peace and justice movements. She finds great joy in being involved with the Fellowship of Reconciliation, Pax Christi, the International Thomas Merton Society, the Florida Coalition for Peace & Justice, and Quakers. Wendy is a member of Jacksonville Friends Meeting and Southeastern Yearly Meeting of The Religious Society of Friends (Quakers).

—Eris A. Northern

A Tree Once Told Me

A tree once told me:
I am like you.
I grow until
I need not make
any more branches
to bear any more leaves.
I grow until I am.
You grow until
you need not live
any more lives
to learn any more lessons.
You grow until you are.

—Wendy Clarissa Geiger, 1981

SOUTHEASTERN YEARLY MEETING PUBLISHING
Quakers in Florida, southeast Georgia, & coastal South Carolina

CPSIA information can be obtained
at www.ICGtesting.com
Printed in the USA
FFOW04n1148090617
36326FF